B. W. Childlaw

I0166158

An historical sketch of Paddy's Run, Butler County, O.

Delivered Saturday, July 30, 1876 by Rev. B. W. Childlaw

B. W. Childlaw

An historical sketch of Paddy's Run, Butler County, O.
Delivered Saturday, July 30, 1876 by Rev. B. W. Childlaw

ISBN/EAN: 9783743328075

Manufactured in Europe, USA, Canada, Australia, Japa

Cover: Foto ©ninafisch / pixelio.de

Manufactured and distributed by brebook publishing software
(www.brebook.com)

B. W. Childlaw

An historical sketch of Paddy's Run, Butler County, O.

"Remember the days of old." Deut. XXXII: 7.

AN HISTORICAL SKETCH

OF

PADDY'S RUN, BUTLER COUNTY, O.

DELIVERED SATURDAY, JULY 30, 1876,

By REV. B. W. CHIDLAW.

HAMILTON TELEGRAPH JOB ROOMS.

To the Reader.

The sole object in preparing this brief historical sketch, is to commemorate the deeds, and to perpetuate the names of the Pioneers of this beautiful valley, the gem of the Miami. In its preparation the writer was aided by his personal knowledge of the original settlers,—by the unfinished manuscript history written by the lamented Roger Williams, and the personal recollections of Mrs. Mary Vaughn and Mrs. Rachel Davies. The interesting sketch of the Schools was furnished by Prof. James A. Clark.

"Remember the days of old." Deut. XXXII: 7.

AN HISTORICAL SKETCH

OF

PADDY'S RUN, BUTLER COUNTY, O.

DELIVERED SATURDAY, JULY 30, 1876,

By REV. B. W. CHIDLAW.

IN the spring of 1795 the good ship "Maria," of Salem, Mass., left the port of Bristol, England, bound for Philadelphia. On board was a company of Welsh emigrants. After a tedious passage of thirteen weeks, the ship reached her destination. Some of the emigrants found employment in and around Philadelphia, others passed on to Cambria Co. Pa., and laid the foundation of a large settlement amid the pines and laurel of the Alleghany Mountains. Others more adventurous found their way to the gates of the North West Territory at Redstone, Old Fort, and thence descended the Monongahela and the Ohio Rivers to the new settlements in the valley of the Miami.

In 1796 Ezekiel Hughes and Edward Bebb, of Llanbrynmair, North Wales, landed at Cincinnati, and spent some time in exploring the new country. The land west of the Miami was not yet surveyed, and until it should be brought into market they squatted on Blue Rock Creek, on the east side of the Miami, opposite to where the village of New Baltimore now stands. Here they were joined by William Gwilym and his wife who followed them from Red Stone.

When the U. S. land was offered for sale in 1801, Ezekiel Hughes bought two sections in what is now Whitewater Township, Hamilton Co. and Edward Bebb bought a half section on the Dry Fork of Whitewater, in what is now Morgan Township, But-

ler Co. This was the first land bought in the township. On the land of his choice Edward Bebb found a squatter named Aaron Cherry, who two or three years previously had built a cabin and cleared a truck patch. The owner of the soil proposed to pay the squatter for his improvements. This honest fair dealing surprised the squatter—it was a new thing in his roving life as a frontiersman. The offer of payment being made and accepted, Aaron Cherry said: "this is the thirteenth time I have squatted, and it is the first time I was ever offered any pay for my improvements." The generosity of Edward Bebb made Aaron Cherry henceforth his trusty friend. This man had a family of sons, celebrated in early times for their horse stealing propensities. One of them met his death when pursued for his crimes. He was a leader of a gang of horse thieves, a terror to the settlers, and refusing to surrender was shot and died in a few days.

After buying land, Mr. Bebb returned to Ebensburg, Pa. and married Mrs. Margaret Owens (formerly Roberts of Llaubrynmair.) This long journey he performed on foot, but his toil was well rewarded in the prize secured. With his young bride he at once left for his Western home. Their son William Bebb (afterwards Governor of Ohio) born December 8th, 1802, was the first white child born in the township. Edward and Margaret Bebb, the first actual settlers, were pillars in society; the latch-string of their cabin always hung out and all new comers received a cordial welcome and timely aid. Mr. Bebb died June 18, 1840, aged 72 years, and Mrs. Bebb Dec. 3d, 1851, aged 77 years, and their graves are among us marked by the loving hands of their sons and daughters, faithful in their testimony of the useful, happy and prolonged life of their honored parents.

William and Morgan Gwilym, brothers from Cevnmaman, South Wales, after spending some time at Red Stone, Pa. came down the Ohio, landed at Cincinnati in 1798, and squatted on Blue Rock Creek near their friends Hughes and Bebb.

While at Red Stone, Pa. they aided in manufacturing the first iron made west of the Allegheny Mountains. William Gwilym was married to Ann Rowlands of Llaubrynmair, North Wales, and in her found a true woman and a faithful wife. Their daughter Rachel (now Mrs. Davies, an honored resident of Paddy's Run.) was born on Blue Rock Creek, now Colerain Township, Hamilton Co. May 28, 1800, and is the first white child born in that township. In 1802 William Gwilym, who had removed to Paddy's Run, Morgan Township, commenced clearing the forest. Morgan Gwilym returned to Red Stone and for two years worked at the furnaces. He invested his earnings in a two-horse wagon and iron castings, which were the first brought to this neighborhood. In 1808 he married Elizabeth Evans, and theirs was one of the first weddings in the settlement. These two families were as polished stones in the foundation of society in this community. Pioneer hospitality abounded in their log cabin as well as in their brick dwellings of later times. William Gwilym died in 1848 aged 82

years, and his wife in 1838, aged 74 years. Morgan Gwilym died in 1845, aged 76 years, and his wife in 1862, aged 78 years.

Andrew Scott and wife settled at the mouth of Paddy's Run about this time. John Vaughan from North Wales bought a half section and settled on it in 1802. He was a man of a quiet spirit and a kind heart. Mr. Vaughan built the first frame barn and the first brick house in the settlement, and they remain though built in 1816. He was industrious and enterprising and his influence for good was widely diffused. He died in 1848 aged 83 years. David Francis and his wife Mary after remaining some time near Philadelphia came west, walking to Pittsburg, then on a "broad horn" down the Ohio to Cincinnati and settled on Paddy's Run in 1802, on a choice piece of land which is now owned by his grandson, Abner Francis, Esq. Deacon Francis died in 1848, aged 76 years and his wife in 1852, aged 78 years. James Nicholas and his wife Mary from South Wales settled in 1803. Mr. Nicholas was the first blacksmith in the neighborhood, and built the first mill on Paddy's Run. In 1831 he removed to Allen Co. Ohio, and was one of the first settlers in that large and prosperous community of Welsh people. He lived to an advanced age. His wife survived him many years and died in 1861, aged 87 years. The Parkinson family, consisting of three brothers, came from Pennsylvania, and bought a half section of land in 1803. The land is now owned by Andrew J. Jones, Thomas F. Jones and Robert Reese. Maurice Jones and his wife Ann, from North Wales, bought land and settled on Paddy's Run in the year 1803, and both died of cholera in the year 1834, within 3 days of each other, much respected and deeply lamented.

During 1803 the families of Jacob Phillis, John and Samuel Harden, Bryson Blackburn, George Drybread, John Howard and Thomas Milholland settled on Paddy's Run and Dry Fork. Blackburn was a blacksmith. His customers had to find the iron and steel which he hammered into axes, hoes, butcher-knives, &c. with a brawny arm and a skillful hand. In 1804 James Shields, a native of Ireland, educated at Glasgow University, Scotland, emigrated with his family from Virginia and purchased a half section of choice land, on which his posterity still reside. Mr. Shields was a man of intelligence and sterling integrity. He served the public as a Representative in the Legislature for nineteen years. These Assemblies of which he was a member met at Chillicothe, Zanesville and Columbus; in 1828 he was elected to Congress, and served his country with fidelity and returned to his constituents a faithful and honored public servant. Mr. Shields travelled from his home on Paddy's Run to our State Capitols and to the Federal city on horseback, and doubtless enjoyed the long and sometimes tedious rides. The evening of his life was spent in the quiet and comfort of his home in the bosom of a loving family, when in 1831 he died, aged over 70 years, leaving a good name and inheritance to his twelve children, and the example of his life for coming generations. In 1804 John Halstead, of North Caroli-

ina, came to the settlement and bought a half section of land, which is still owned and occupied by his descendants. Mr. Halstead lived to see his eightieth year and died in 1855. Mrs. Halstead, a most exemplary woman and good neighbor, died in 1840, aged 66 years. Abel and Thomas Appleton with their families settled on the half section of land on which some of their descendants still live. Thomas died in 1845, aged 72 years, and his wife Abigail aged 70 years soon afterward. Abel Appleton died in 1834, aged 62 years, and his wife Elizabeth long survived him, departing in peace at the advanced age of 89 years.

From 1806 until the close of the war of 1812, the following families came into the settlement: William Evans and family from North Wales settled on the hill west of Dry Fork. Mr. Evans died in 1822, aged 66 years. William Jenkins and family from Virginia settled on Dry Fork. Mr. Jenkins and his wife died at an advanced age. Two brothers, King and Alexander DeArmond, natives of Pennsylvania, settled, the one on Paddy's Run and the other on Dry Fork, lived to a good old age, and left a numerous posterity, many of whom are still living in the township. Rev. Michael Bottenberg from Maryland, a minister of the United Brethren Church, a faithful and honored servant of God; many of his descendants are among us to-day. John Merring, a son-in-law of Mr. Bottenberg came at the same time, and settled on the land now occupied by his son-in-law Evan Evans, Esq. Robert Mahaffy from Pennsylvania, with a large family settled on the hill between Paddy's Run and Dry Fork. Rev. Hezekiah Shaw, a son-in-law of John Halstead, a laborious minister of the Gospel, resided in the neighborhood and devoted his time to the service of the Methodist Episcopal Church, traveling extensive circuits, useful and honored in his laborious and self-sacrificing duties as a pioneer herald of the Cross. William D. Jones from Wales settled near Mr. Shields and opened the first mercantile house in the township. Peter Youmans and his family from New Jersey, settled on the farm where he lived for many years, a faithful christian and a genial neighbor. He died in 1837 aged 60, and Mrs. Youmans in 1874 aged 93. Ephraim Carmack from Maryland, brought with him a team of eight horses and a genuine Conestoga wagon. He settled where Robert Reese now lives. He was a natural born teamster and distinguished in his cherished avocation. He was also a "mighty hunter" and seldom returned from his excursions without bringing many trophies of his skill in the chase. He removed with his family to Mercer Co. and was among the early Pioneers in that section. In 1817 Rev. Rees Lloyd and family came from Ebensburg. Pa. and bought land on the hill between Paddy's Run and Dry Fork. His life and labors will be considered in the history of the church. In 1818 a new era of emigration from Wales was inaugurated, and large accessions made to the population and resources of the settlement. During the year the following families, chiefly from Montgomeryshire, North Wales made this valley their homes: John C. Jones and Jane

his wife, Evan and Jane Morris, John and Jane Breese, Richard Jones and wife, William Davis and wife, (the parents of the distinguished physicians John and William B. Davis, now of Cincinnati,) George and Catherine Williams, Evan and Mary Humphreys, Griffith Breese and wife and Humphrey Evans and wife. Connected with these families were a number of adult unmarried persons, among them Francis Jones, who married Elizabeth Francis, John Evans (still surviving at the age of 81 years) who married Miss Sarah Nicholas; Deacon David Jones who married Mrs Mary Humphreys; John Swancott who married Miss Mary Jones: David Davies who married Miss Rachel Gwilym. The families of Evan Owens, Evan Davies and Tubal Jones, from Cardiganshire, South Wales, were added to the families of this valley at this time. From 1820 to 1830 many emigrants from Wales found their way to Paddy's Run, adding to the religious and industrial prosperity of the neighborhood. Among them were Deacon Hugh Williams from Anglesea, North Wales, who married Mrs. Eliza Gwilym Francis, who is with us this day. Joseph Griffiths and Jane his wife with a large family of sons and daughters from Carno, North Wales, who in 1837 removed to Allen County, Ohio. Henry Davis from Ebensburg, Pa., who married Miss Mary Evans; Thomas Watkins, who married Miss Jane Evans; David Roberts, who married Miss Annie Nicholas; Rowland Jones and wife; John Jones who married Miss Jane Gwilym. In 1832 these families with James Nicholas and family became the pioneer settlers of the large and prosperous Welsh community now found in Allen Co. Ohio.

Thus we have endeavored to recall the names of the early pioneer families of Morgan Township, especially of the valley of Paddy's Run—families whose record for industry, frugality, probity hospitality, patriotism and religion is a rich legacy to their posterity and to the entire community.

The facts and incidents connected with life in the cabin and toil in the clearing are worthy of remembrance. The first settlers were men of sound judgment and clear perception. After selecting the land and entering it at the land office, they fixed upon the spot amid the unbroken forest where they would build their cabin, and it is evidence of the wisdom of their selections that, in almost every instance, the beautiful dwellings adorning the valley and its hillsides are located on the identical spots selected over sixty years ago. After selecting the location for a home, the site was cleared, logs chopped, clapboards rived and the puncheons hewed. The cabin was then raised, all the neighbors assisting; four corner men, expert choppers, on the building, the rest rolling up the logs; men and women uniting their strength kept the corner men busy receiving the logs, chopping the notch and hewing the saddle. Two days finished the job; oil papered windows, doors of clapboards hung on wooden hinges; the floors laid with smooth hewed puncheons; the cracks chunked and daubed; the chimney built of wood and mud—the home of the pioneer was finished and occupied.

The furniture was largely made by the help of the axe, drawing knife and augur, and of whatever articles the settler brought with him or purchased in the village of Cincinnati. The question what shall we eat and what shall we drink they answered by using the articles of subsistence that a kind Providence brought in their way. The forest abounded in game, and the river in fish; sugar and honey they obtained from the forest, and their truck patches furnished vegetables; soon their industry enabled them to husk corn and harvest wheat; pork and poultry contributed to their supplies, and their tables were loaded with good things. Instead of "store tea" they had sassafras and spicewood, delicious and aromatic. None ever suffered for the want of daily food, and in a few years all the necessaries and comforts of life abounded.

In early times our pioneer ancestors were compelled to use ingenuity as well as invention in providing clothing. Buckskin furnished material for moccasons and fringed hunting shirts, but in a few years sheep were introduced and flax sown; these the women spun, wove and cut, and made substantial and comfortable garments; the bark of trees was used in coloring, and there was no lack of taste or subjection to the tyranny of fashion in the art of dress-making. Sun-bonnets made of pasteboard and a yard of calico were fashionable for forty years.

ROADS.

For several years "blazed" tracks or paths, with the underbrush removed, answered the purpose for traveling from cabin to cabin. After the county road had been laid out and opened from Cincinnati to the Miami, and the regions beyond in 1805, and Morgan Gwilym brought the first wagon into the township, a new era of transportation dawned on the new country. For many years the settlers took the produce of their fields, poultry yards and dairies to Cincinnati on pack horses. At an early day, Paddy's Run butter commanded a quick sale and a premium in lower market, then the business center of the Queen City. Hospitality and sociability were cardinal virtues among the pioneers. Their raisings, log-rollings, corn-huskings and harvestings; their chopping frolics, quiltings and wool pickings are the memorials of their readiness to help each other. In the absence of a factory, their home-made woollens were fulled by using a trough—a row of men on one side and of women on the other using their feet, the soap and water served a good purpose, and the process was eminently successful. Whisky made in the one-horse distilleries of the day, free from adulterations, was used on these occasions, but seldom to excess. Some knight of the fiddle being present, the youth wound up the labors of the day with dancing. The "Race Lane" is suggestive of horse racing, and shooting matches, when the best marksman would carry off the turkeys, were the common sports of the day.

The year 1811 was memorable for the appearance of a wonderful comet. During the summer a fearful pestilence visited the settlement, and nearly all who were smitten by the disease died. It was called the "cold plague." After the pestilence came a terrible hail storm, the ground was covered with pieces of ice of irregular shape, some of them measuring six inches in circumference. In 1812 an earthquake convulsed the settlement and filled the hearts of the people with terror; many of our older citizens remember the shocks, having felt them in their own persons. These wonderful visitations of Providence produced a marked effect on the people, not of superstitious awe, but a devout acknowledgment of the rulings of Divine Providence.

THE WAR OF 1812.

In 1813 a company of volunteers was raised in Morgan Township under the command of Capt. W. D. Jones. The house of John Vaughan was the place of rendezvous. The patriotism and liberality of the settlers was manifested in an abundant supply of blankets and subsistence for the use of the volunteers. They marched with other troops to the relief of Gen. Hull, then beleaguered by the British at Detroit. On their way through the forest they suffered for food; near Fort Wayne, Ind. they captured three bushels of parched corn in bark boxes secreted by the Indians, and on this they subsisted until they reached the Fort. Hull having surrendered they returned. One of their number, Samuel Harding, died of disease contracted in the service. In 1861 when our National life was imperiled by armed traitors, thirty-eight volunteers from this township enlisted in the 5th O. V. Cavalry, and during the war a large number entered the army, all rendering their country in the time of its need heroic and important service. Some laid down their lives on the battle field and others have suffered from wounds and disease. The war record of Morgan Township is a noble tribute to the loyalty and heroism of its inhabitants, and the names and memory of the brave soldiers should be held in everlasting remembrance.

THE FIRST DEATH

in the township is said to have been a daughter of Benjamin James, a squatter on Dry Fork, and resulted from the bite of a rattlesnake at the spring. A coffin was made by splitting a black walnut log and dressing it with a broadaxe and drawing knife. These slabs were fastened with wooden pins; the body laid in this rude casket was carried by loving hands to the first grave dug in the neighborhood at the foot of what is now known as "Race Lane." Mrs. Blackburn, mother of William Blackburn, was the first who died on Paddy's Run, and her remains were buried in

the woods on the hill west of where Mrs. Margaret Sefton now resides. A pen of logs surrounds it, and some of us have seen it.

EARLY MECHANICS.

A clock case now owned by Mrs. Mary Vaughan, made for her father, Edward Bebb, by Stephen Hayden in 1804, shows the ingenuity and taste of this pioneer cabinet-maker. It is made of cherry slabs, dressed as best he could, overcoming the want of saw mills with a whip saw. Stephen Hayden with such tools as he had, made a beautiful and neatly ornamented clock case worthy of a place in the great Centennial Exhibit at Philadelphia. For over seventy years it has been the cosy home of a brass clock which Mrs. Bebb brought from Wales seventy-nine years ago. The face of the clock is 12 by 12 inches, but when the case was made the Cincinnati market could not furnish a piece of glass large enough to cover it. The glass is in two pieces, neatly joined by the hand of the skillful mechanic. This venerable clock (good as new after all its ticking in four score years,) was a great curiosity to the Indians who frequently visited Mr. Bebb's cabin. He would make the clock strike around in their hearing, but the children of the forest must have the cabin door open, that in case of danger they might seek safety in flight. Capt. William D. Jones brought the first stock of goods into the township on a pack-horse, and opened a place of business near where the turnpike crosses Paddy's Run. His business was conducted chiefly on a bartering basis, as specie was very scarce. The first physicians were Drs. Sloan and Millikin, of Hamilton, and Dr. Crookshank, of Harrison. They practiced as early as 1806, and were eminent in their profession and useful in the community. The township was organized in 1811, but in 1808 Maxwell Parkinson officiated as Justice of the Peace, but by what authority is unknown—probably appointed by the Governor. After the organization of the township, the citizens elected King DeArmond, Wm. D. Jones, Hugh Smith, Wm. Jenkins, Wm. Bebb, Ephraim Carmack and others to this office.

THE LIBRARY.

The men who laid the foundations of society in these beautiful valleys were intelligent, and the firm friends of knowledge. In 1821 a bill was passed in the Ohio Legislature incorporating the "Union Library Association of Morgan and Crosby Townships." The shares cost $3, and sixty-five were taken. The books purchased were standard works on history, morals and science. The Library was kept at Smith's Mill on Dry Fork, and the shareholders assiduously improved their opportunities to read.

THE ASIATIC CHOLERA

in a malignant type visited the neighborhood in 1834, especially

the eastern side of the valley of Paddy's Run. About sixty persons, mostly adults, died during the prevalence of the epidemic which continued about three weeks. Some families were almost swept away by the power of the deadly pestilence, and there was scarcely a house which the angel of death did not visit. In 1852 the flux prevailed as an epidemic, and in two weeks twenty died of the disease. On the 16th of November, 1854, a terrible calamity was occasioned by the fall of the steeple of this church. Six valuable lives were lost—Nathaniel Jones and Robert Jones were instantly killed; on the next day John C. Jones, Esq., aged 58, died from injuries received. His death was a great loss to his family, the church and the community. In a month, Jacob Phillis, the contractor died, and after lingering several weeks Thomas Jones and Elias Williamson died. In 1856 Robert Griffiths and his family, after residing several years on Paddy's Run beloved and respected, left for Missouri. They embarked at Cincinnati on the steamer "Nannie Byers." Near Madison, Ind. the boat sunk, and this worthy family, father, mother, four adult children and a son-in-law lost their lives in the turbid waters of the Ohio. Their remains were recovered and buried in the old graveyard, in the presence of an immense concourse of sorrowing friends.

GRAVE YARDS.

The oldest in the township was located on the west side of Camp Run near its mouth; all traces of this first burial place are obliterated. John Halstead and Ephraim Carmack opened graveyards on their farms, which the neighborhood used for many years. In 1821, John Vaughan and Morgan Gwilym donated the lot for meeting house and graveyard, and until 1867, when the new cemetery was opened, this was the place where the dead found a sepulcher, and where nearly all the old settlers have been buried.

RELIGIOUS HISTORY.

Several of the pioneer settlers were members of churches, and all of them respected the christian religion. They entered these unbroken forests with an open bible held in high estimation—they honored the Sabbath day and regarded Christianity and its institutions as of first importance in the moral and material prosperity of the settlement. With these convictions they early and kindly opened their cabin doors and cordially welcomed any minister of the gospel whose zeal and faithfulness led him to the neighborhood. The first minister that unfurled the gospel banner in the settlement was Rev. John W. Browne, of Cincinnati, a Congregationalist from England. He preached at the houses of Edward Bebb on Dry Fork; Andrew Scott, at the mouth of Paddy's Run; John Vaughan on Paddy's Run, and David Lee on Lee's creek. All the settlers through these localities attended and appreciated his ministry. In July 1803, at the house of David Lee, a com-

mittee consisting of Mr. Browne, Asa Kitchel, A. Scott, Joab Comstock and David Cunningham was appointed to draft a constitution and articles of faith for the proposed religious society and present it before the people. On Sept. 3, 1803, at the house of John Templeton, on Dry Fork, near New Haven, the report of the committee was adopted. The society was called "The Whitewater Congregational Church;" its doctrinal basis;evangelical but not sectarian. Its first members were Benjamin McCarty, Asa Kitchel, Joab Comstock, Andrew Scott, Margaret Bebb, Ezekiel Hughes, William and Ann Gwilym, David and Mary Francis. In this little company of believers, as sheep scattered in the wilderness, were members of the body of Christ, his friends and followers from Scotland, Ireland, Wales and New England. One in Christ, they cordially united in Him, and organized a New Testament Church. In 1804, at the house of John Bennefield, in Crosby township, Hamilton Co. according to previous arrangement, Mr. Browne was ordained to preach the gospel and administer the ordinances of the church. The record shows that the church appointed a committee of its own members to set apart this brother to the sacred office and work of the ministry. The service of ordaining him was simple and in accord with their views of bible teaching, and recognized as valid as if performed with pomp and show within the walls of a Cathedral, by men appointed and vested with authority by church and state. The little flock thus folded, and in the care of the Pastor, meeting on the Sabbath from cabin to cabin, and often with a large congregation, worshipping God in the grove beneath the shade of the forest trees, grew and multiplied, and the hand of the Lord was with his people. In 1810 or 1811 Mr. Browne lost his life in the Little Miami River, on his way to an appointment in Clermont Co. His death was a great loss to the church and the community. From 1810 to 1817 the records of the church are lost. Without a meeting-house and without regular preaching, the church held together, and its influence on the side of morality and religion, of social and intellectual culture continued; its light ceased not to burn. REV. REES LLOYD, of Ebensburg, Pa., (who with his wife and children were passengers on the "Maria" in 1795,) was invited to accept the pastorate of the church, to preach in Welsh and English. He entered upon his labors in 1817, preaching in dwelling houses and gathering good congregations. In 1820 REV. THOMAS THOMAS, of Welsh parentage, but a native of England, pastor of a Congregational church, at Chelmsford, Eng. emigrated to this country with his family, and was invited as co-pastor with Mr. Lloyd. He was a good scholar, an able expounder of the Holy Scriptures, and an eloquent preacher. His labors in this and the surrounding neighborhoods greatly advanced the cause of religion. Mr. Lloyd gave up the pastorate of the church, and Mr. Thomas continued, and also established a school which gained much celebrity. In 1823 Matthias Ollis and Roger Sargent were chosen deacons. Mr. Thomas preached in his school room, in

dwelling houses and in the wagon shop of David Jones, and when the weather was favorable in the open air, beneath a grove of sugar trees, where Mrs. Eliza Williams now resides. The want of a house of worship was a great necessity, and indeed a hindrance to the permanent growth and spiritual prosperity of the church. The people, led by their Pastor, had a heart to work, and in 1823 the old meeting-house was commenced, the foundations 43 by 30 feet were laid, and the brick burnt. The next year the walls were erected and the building enclosed. In 1825, temporary seats, and a pulpit made of two upright scantling and a board, furnished the house of the Lord. The first service within its walls was the funeral of Mrs. Ruth Vaughan.

In 1827 Mr. Thomas gave up the care of the church, and accepted a call to the pastorate of the Presbyterian church, at Venice, O., where he labored successfully until his death in 1831, and he was buried among his people honored and beloved. Mr. Lloyd also retired from the active work of the ministry, and died in 1838, aged 80 years, and his remains interred in a graveyard adjoining the "Hickory Chapel" near Daniel Otto's house, on the hill between Paddy's Run and Dry Fork. In July 1828, Rev. Thomas G. Roberts, of Ebensburg, Pa., entered upon the pastoral office in this church, preaching in both languages. Under his labors the church prospered, but failing health made it necessary for him to return to his home in Pennsylvania in the year 1831. Rev. Evan Roberts, of Steuben, N. Y. came to the neighborhood, and preached several months, then returned and died in 1834. In 1836, Rev. B. W. Chidlaw, of Radnor, Ohio, a student at the Miami University, who had preached in the neighborhood for over a year, was called to the pastorate. He was ordained in May, 1836, Rev. R. H. Bishop, D. D. President of the University presiding. Rev. Prof. J. W. Scott, D. D. delivered a charge to the people, and Rev. S. Scovill, of Harrison, a charge to the young pastor. Mr. Chidlaw continued his ministry for seven years, the church growing in numbers and spirituality, and the Sabbath School work of the church in the surrounding neighborhoods was greatly extended. He entered the service of the American S. S. Union and continues in it to this day. In 1843, Rev. Ellis Howell, from England, entered upon the work of the ministry, and continued several years. He is now pastor of the Presbyterian church, at Reily, O. He was followed by Rev. Jos. H. Jones, from South Wales, an earnest, faithful servant of God, now ending a useful and prolonged life in his home in Randolph Co. Ind. Since that time, Rev. James M. Pryse, now laboring in Minnesota; Rev. D. W. Wilson, now in Tenn.; Rev. J. M. Thomas, now in Pomeroy, Ohio; Rev. H. R. Price, whose long life and useful ministry closed so recently; Rev. J. C. Thompson and Rev. George Candee, both still living and laboring in Northern Ohio, have had the pastoral care of the church. Rev. John L. Davies, a graduate of Marietta College, and a student at Lane Seminary, was ordained by the

Conference of Southern Ohio, in Gallia Co. and entered upon his work as pastor a few months ago with prospects of success in his important work.

DEACONS OF THE CHURCH.

The brethren called to the office of Deacons were men of "honest report, full of the Holy Ghost and wisdom." Their names and services deserve our recall, and a warm place in the memory of the present generation. Of Joab Comstock, Asa Kitchel, Matthias Ollis and Roger Sargent, the time of their death, their age and place of burial we have no information. David Francis many of us knew and esteemed highly for his work's sake. He died in 1848, aged 76 years. David Jones, whose recent death the entire community deplores, was a stern steadfast disciple of the Lord Jesus Christ—a pillar in the church, strong in the faith and faithful in duty. John Merring and Hugh Williams in the vigor of their days were chosen deacons, and they failed not in the conscientious and faithful discharge of their duties. Brother Merring, by the kick of a horse in his door-yard, was called from the labors of life to the rest of heaven. His sudden death was generally deplored, and his memory is fragrant unto this day. He died in 1849. Hugh Williams, in his quiet and genial way, showed his love for the church and his interest in its prosperity. A devoted student of the Scriptures, he was rooted and grounded in the faith. He died in peace March 7th, 1870, aged 64 years, and left to his family and to the church, the inheritance of a good name and devoted piety.

In 1848, David Davies was elected to the office of a Deacon. and faithfully discharged its duties until his death in 1855, aged 62 years. The same year William Jones received and accepted a call to the Deacon-ship. He was a man of prayer, mighty in the Scriptures and full of humble devotion to his work. He died in 1858, aged 64 years. John Gibbon served with fidelity in the office of a Deacon until he removed to Illinois, where he still resides. Thos. F. Jones, Abner Francis and Robert Reese are now the acting Deacons of the church, loving Zion and laboring for its prosperity. The members of the church now number one hundred and fifty, and the attendance on the worship of God on the Sabbath is large. The inhabitants of this vicinity have always been distinguished for their observance of the Sabbath, their high estimate and profound reverence for the Holy Bible, and their attendance on the ministry of the Gospel. From the early days when the tabernacle of God was movable, and fondly welcomed into the log cabins of the godly pioneers, the religious element in its purity and power, in moulding the highest type of christian civilization, has been cherished and supported in this community. The early embodiment of the religious life and character of the original settlers into a church organization, founded on the broad and sure foundation of our common christianity, has secured

innumerable blessings to the generations following. True to its principles of christian unity and co-operation, intolerance and bigotry blighted not this garden of the Lord. One strong and united church, and not a half dozen sectarian organizations weak and powerless for doing good, is the glory and power of Zion on this hill of the Lord to-day. With this spirit of love and labor, of wisdom and mutual confidence, they cohered and formed the church whose history abounds in testimonials of the Divine favor and in fulfillment of the promises of a covenant-keeping God. The liberality of the church in building two houses of worship both standing to-day in the support of the gospel at home, and in sending it abroad from the time when a part of the salary of its first pastor was paid in grain, delivered at his home in Cincinnati, has never failed. Liberal bequests were made by Deacon Hugh Williams and William Jones to the American Bible Society, and the American Missionary Society. Miss Ann Evans, Deacon David Francis and Mrs. Elizabeth Gwilym have bequeathed a generous sum for the support of the gospel in this church. The fund is safely invested and the interest available for the purposes designed.

THE FIRST SABBATH SCHOOL

was organized in 1819, in a private house and superintended by Benjamin Lloyd. The attendance of the youth and adults was good, and much interest excited in the study of the Bible and committing verses to memory. After the arrival of Rev. Mr. Thomas and his family in 1821, a new life was infused into the Sabbath School, and a supply of books published by the American S. S. Union secured. These books were very generally read and found to be very useful. The school continued until now and has been very useful to the church and neighborhood. It now numbers one hundred and fifty scholars, with a band of twenty faithful teachers under the supervision of Deacon Abner Francis. The influence and labor of the pastor, Rev. J. L. Davies, in encouraging the teachers and scholars to study the Scriptures, is doing much to elevate the standard and the methods of teaching, and in promoting the general interests of the good work. For over fifty years the Sabbath School with its Divine text book, its sacred toleration and oral instruction, has been a great blessing to the community. For many years a school held in the old meeting house was conducted in the Welsh language which the adult population greatly enjoyed. As the Welsh language declined the school was given up a few years ago, but the record of its usefulness is treasured on high.

PRAYER MEETINGS

and church meetings have a history coeval with the church. Every week, generally on Thursday evening, a goodly attendance of adults and youth meet for prayer and praise. For many years

a weekly conference, a society meeting, was held in the Welsh language, a blessed means of grace developing and strengthening the religious life and experience of all that attended. A monthly meeting of the church for the transaction of business has been held from the beginning. The sacrament of the Lord's Supper is administered monthly, accompanied with special religious services, rendering the occasion a spiritual privilege highly enjoyed by the church. For many years the female members of the church and congregation have sustained a weekly prayer meeting in the English language, which has awakened a deep religious interest and called out much christian work in behalf of temperance, and every other good work and word.

CHURCH CLERKS. 1818082

The records of the church, embodying much valuable and interesting history, have been kept by the following brethren: James Scott was appointed in 1804, and served many years. From 1820 to 1827 the records are signed by the pastor, Rev. T. Thomas. In 1828 Evan Davies, a faithful common school teacher, was chosen clerk, and continued in office for twelve years until he removed to take charge of the Public Schools of Hamilton. In 1837 Deacon David Davies was appointed, and served faithfully until he was succeeded by Thomas F. Jones in 1849. Bro. Jones, gifted in the use of the pen, kept the records until he was succeeded by Griffith Morris in 1871, who still serves in this office.

THE YOUNG MEN OF PADDY'S RUN.

Rev. Thomas E. Thomas, D. D. graduated at the Miami University, Oxford, Ohio, in 1834, entered the ministry in 1836 pastor of the Presbyterian church at Harrison, O., afterward at Hamilton and Dayton. He closed his useful life in 1875, when serving the church as Professor in Lane Theological Seminary. He was a profound scholar, an able expositor of the Holy Scriptures and an eloquent preacher. Alfred Thomas graduated at the same University in 1838, entered the profession of law, and now resides in Washington, D. C. where he holds an important position in the Law Department of the U. S. Treasury. Rev. Abner Jones, son of Francis Jones, graduated at Oxford in 1858, and at Lane Seminary in 1861. He was pastor of the Congregational church of Columbia, and New Albany, Licking Co. Ohio. In 1864 he responded to the call of his country and entered the service as a christian hero. He died at Alexandria, D. C. and his remains were brought home to rest in the new cemetery. Rev. W. Mark Williams, son of Hugh Williams, graduated at Oxford in 1858 and at Lane Seminary in 1861. After an acceptable and useful ministry of two years, he with his wife embarked under the auspices of the American Board of Commissioners for foreign missions for China, where he remains in charge of the Mission of Kalgan, in the northern part of the empire.

Rev. Thomas McClelland and his brother Samuel, sons of Isaac McClelland, graduated at Oxford. The former is pastor of the Presbyterian church at Chester, Ohio, and the latter doing good service as an educator. Oliver Jones, son of Deacon Thomas F. Jones, and Griffin M. Shaw, son of Dr. Shaw, graduated at Wabash College, Ind. Mr. Jones is a successful teacher, and Mr. Shaw died in 1873. Roger Williams, son of Hugh Williams, graduated at Oxford in 1872, went to Europe the following year, lost his health and with much difficulty came home to die. He was preparing for the life of a journalist, but his early death cut off his purposes and his sun went down while it was yet noon. Several of the young men of this neighborhood without a University education have made their mark in the world in professional life. Among them we note Evan Morris, a civil engineer; the new church was built under his supervision and several important turnpikes show his skill and faithfulness in his profession. Dr. Griffin Shaw entered the medical profession and was greatly esteemed in the community, and his early death was universally lamented. Murat Halstead, son of Col. Griffin Halstead, has for many years edited the Cincinnati *Commercial* one of the leading newspapers of our country. Mr. Halstead is esteemed as one of the first journalists of our land. Many of the young women of Paddy's Run deserve great credit for their noble ambition to obtain an education, and for the use they have made of their scholarship and talents in their devotion to the work of life in its highest forms of usefulness and true womanhood.

SKETCH OF THE SCHOOLS.

The first school in the township was in a log school-house built in 1807, on land now owned by Thos. Shields, Esq. and taught by Miss Polly Wiley. Her salary was seventy-five cents a week, boarding around. She taught her twenty scholars reading and spelling. She was succeeded by a Mr. Jenkins in 1808. He was noted for his method of teaching morals and manners to his pupils. Before dismissing them at noon, he collected them with their dinner around a large table in the center of the room, and after asking a blessing upon the meal, he acted as "Autocrat of the dinner table," requiring silent attention from all. In 1809 another school was begun in a rented log cabin, on Dry Fork, in the western part of the township. Here Adam Mow taught a subscription school at $1.50 per scholar, for a term of three months.

In 1810 the citizens of this place met together and built a log cabin school house with cat and clay chimney, wooden latch, slab benches, board roof and two small windows; but provided with no black-board, maps, globe or charts. Here the children were taught to spell in Dilworth's spelling book, and to read in the New Testament, Bunyan's Pilgrim's Progress and American Preceptor, and to write, and to cipher in Bennet's and Pike's Arithmetics, graduating at the "rule of three." The qualifica-

tions of the teacher were decided by those appointed to employ teachers, according to reputation, or recommendation, or decided characteristics, as good penmanship, ability in arithmetic, or austerity in manner and discipline.

In this way the schools were kept during three or four months of each year, no change being made except a change of teachers occasionally, until 1819, when David Lloyd, a graduate from Philadelphia, was employed to teach. He introduced grammar and geography into the schools, and classified his pupils in these branches and in arithmetic. Before this, each pupil recited by himself, or rather did not recite at all. He was an eccentric man, having spent most of his life in a vain effort to invent perpetual motion. He taught for the same wages as his predecessors, and collected his tuition from his patrons. The general government had made some provision to help the schools before this, by appropriating the land in section sixteen of each township for this purpose. This land was leased for a series of years by the Township Trustees, to be put under cultivation, and now part of it was rented for one-third grain rent, which amounted to twenty or thirty bushels of corn, worth ten or twelve cents per bushel. This plan of renting the land for grain rent was continued until the land was considerably run down, when most of it was sold, and the interest of the money divided, pro rata, among the schools.

In 1821, in addition to the Common School, Rev. Thomas Thomas, father of the late T. E. Thomas, D. D., of Lane Theological Seminary, established a High School and boarding school, in which he taught, for a series of years, advanced pupils in grammar, geography, arithmetic, algebra and geometry. This was a great impetus to the growth of the educational spirit of the community, and in the same year the "Union Library Association of Morgan and Crosby" was formed and chartered by the Legislature, and approved by the Supreme Court, Judge Burnet and Judge McLain ratifying the articles. In this library were such books as Plutarch's Lives, Rollin's Ancient History, Josephus, Mungo Park's travels, Lewis and Clark, Campbell on the Miracles, Paley's Evidences of Christianity, Butler's Analogy, &c., and by examining the librarian's record, we find that these books were drawn out and read by almost every citizen of the two townships; and thus the intelligence of the people was greatly increased, and a desire for improvement was awakened in both old and young. And this desire has been growing ever since, so that when the schools were organized under the State law in 1826, the people were eager to avail themselves of its advantages. A new school house was built, and William Bebb, who became Governor of Ohio in 1846, was the first teacher employed under the State law. He taught two years and then taught High School four years, when he went to Hamilton and studied and practiced law until he was elected Governor. We had township examiners to decide upon the qualifications of teachers as early as 1825. The Hon. James Shields, who had been nineteen years a member of the

Ohio Legislature, and who was afterwards in 1829, a member of Congress, was the first examiner. Excepting Professor McGuffey, he was perhaps the best scholar and most influential man in the county, taking a leading part in all the educational enterprises. He was educated at Glasgow, Scotland. He examined Governor Bebb, Evan Davies and other noted teachers. From 1828 to 1832, Governor Bebb was township examiner. Evan Davies taught here for six or seven years, commencing in 1830. He was for forty years one of the most prominent educators of Butler county, being County Examiner from 1840 to 1869. After Mr. Bebb, the Rev. Benjamin Lloyd and Rev. B. W. Chidlaw, well known as a veteran worker in the American Sunday School Union and in Ohio as a Trustee of the Reform Farm School at Lancaster, Ohio, were Township Examiners. From 1837 to 1840, Mr. Chidlaw taught High School here with great success.

These eminent teachers gave a good education to those who have since furnished pupils and teachers for our schools. Among the most noted in the Rev. Thomas Thomas's school we might mention Charles Selden, author of Selden's Book-keeping, and the late T. E. Thomas, D. D., of Lane Theological Seminary, who is the author of one of the best works on homiletics in the English language. In Governor Bebb's school we mention William Dennison, who became Governor of Ohio in 1861, Hon. G. M. Shaw, of Indiana, and Hon. Daniel Shaw, a member of the first legislature of Louisiana after the late rebellion. He was Sheriff of Grant parish, and had charge of the colored troops at the time of the Colfax massacre, and Hon. Peter Melindy, one of the most prominent Republican politicians in Iowa. These schools were patronized by many of the most wealthy families in Cincinnati and the Southern States. Mr. Evan Davies built up and popularized the Common Schools, and prepared pupils for the High School, teaching some of the higher branches himself in the public schools, so that Mr. Chidlaw's school had more of a home influence. He taught more on the modern plan, introducing the modern improvements of black-board, charts, &c. He prepared some eminently successful teachers, among whom we may mention T. F. Jones, Griffith Morris, Evan Morris and M. R. Shields. These gentlemen conducted the schools here and in the neighboring villages with great success for several years. Mr. M. R. Shields afterwards filled the office of County Surveyor very successfully, in Butler county, for a number of years. Mr. Evan Morris graduated in civil engineering in the College of Cincinnati, under Professor Mitchell, a distinguished mathematician and astronomer. Some distinguished editors also attended Mr. Chidlaw's school, the best known of whom is Murat Halstead, the editor and publisher of the Cincinnati Daily *Commercial*, whose father, Colonel Griffin Halstead, still lives here.

Under the management of these excellent teachers the public schools were very prosperous, and wages were increased from $12 to $25, and afterwards to $30 per month. In 1852 or 1853 a

new library association was formed, and about one thousand volumes of choice standard works were purchased for it, which were free to the people to read.

Thus it will be seen that up to this time, this place has shown a praiseworthy example in educational progress. Since this time we have had some ups and downs, and individual failures, such as occur almost everywhere. But it is not our province to speak of these, but rather to show the general progress that has been made. No one should suppose that every teacher has been a success because we do not take pains to point out the failures that have been made, though we feel free to say that these have been few and far between.

In 1858 the Academy, or High School, was organized on a more permanent basis. Twelve of the most prominent citizens were appointed as Directors, who made themselves responsible for the payment of all expenses connected with the school, the funds for which were mainly derived from tuition, and they employed David McClung, afterwards Judge McClung, as Principal, at a salary of $3.00 per day. At this time black-boards, wall maps, globes, charts, instruments and all the modern appliances to facilitate teaching were systematically used. The Public School was also at this time divided into two departments, primary and secondary. The Misses Atherton, three sisters who received their preparatory education here, and finished their studies at the Western Seminary at Oxford, and Michael Jones, of this place, were all very popular teachers in the public schools, and were employed for several years. In the High School the teachers were changed often, though most of the teachers were men of ability, being nearly all graduates of college, and all professional teachers, as the rules of the Company required that none but professional teachers should be employed. Yet the colleges had given them good training, and were not at fault, for most of them left their situation here because they obtained better situations elsewhere.

Of the noted teachers we mention two, Rev. David Wilson, who had been a missionary in Syria for fifteen years, a man of great ability and energy and success as a missionary, preacher and teacher, and Rev. Mark Williams, a graduate of Miami University, and of Lane Theological Seminary, who has been for the past ten years a missionary at Kalgan, China, sent out by the American Board. He was prepared for college here.

A large number of the Principals in the High School here, are now filling high professional positions as preachers, lawyers and doctors.

In 1865 James A. Clark, the present Principal of the Graded Schools, was employed as Principal of the High School. Under his management the school was quite successful. But in order that both the High School and the Public School might be more efficient, it was necessary that they should be united, and the people felt this. And so, after the Act of the Legislature, passed

April 9, 1867, being an Act for the organization of Special School Districts, the leaven of enthusiasm so pervaded the whole community that they were unanimous in their vote to avail themselves of the benefits of this law. And on December 10th, 1869, the New London Special School was organized, and Messrs. Jacob Scheel, Evan Evans and Thomas Appleton were the first Board appointed under this Act. They employed as Principal Samuel McClelland, a former pupil of the High School, and graduate of Miami University, and also a member of the present Board of Examiners of Butler county. But at this time the school was not thoroughly graded and classified, for want of suitable rooms.

In 1871 a large and beautiful lot of about three acres was purchased, and a commodious brick school house was erected, containing four departments furnished in modern style, the whole costing about thirteen thousand dollars.

At that time the basis of the present system of classification was formed by Miss Florence Shafer (the only lady teacher ever employed in the High School,) and the three members of the Board then acting, viz: Messrs. Griffith Morris, Abner Francis and Evan Evans, the first two being men of more than ordinary scholarship and experience as teachers, and all three men of wealth and influence; and above all, thoroughly in earnest in their efforts to build up a good school. Three grades were formed, Primary, Intermediate and High School. In 1872 James A. Clark, former Principal of the High School, was employed as Principal; and since that time much has been done with the co-operation of the Board and citizens, to establish a course of study and system of education and mental training that would best prepare our youth for citizenship and the duties of life.

We have had for the past five years an enumeration of about one hundred and ninety pupils of school age in the district, which is two by three miles, the population being about stationary. We have enrolled each year, since 1872, about one hundred and eighty-five pupils, including about twenty pupils each year who attended from other places, and who pay tuition at the rate of thirty dollars for forty weeks in the High School. And we could have double this number if we were prepared to accommodate them. A great many pupils attend the High School to prepare for teaching, and many young gentlemen and ladies to prepare for college.

It must not be inferred from what has been said of the young men of Paddy's Run, that they have surpassed the young women; for as great a number have graduated with honor, and have filled, and are still filling high positions in the work of education and of the church.

The generations yet to come, in the example of their godly ancestors, will have a rich legacy. A good name untarnished— brain and muscle embodied in useful industry, a life of sound morality and true religion is a grand inheritance and worthy of the highest appreciation. A sacred trust rests upon the present generation to hold and transmit the inheritance of the Pioneer fathers, their broad and productive acres, the institutions of education, morality and religion, which they established and so faithfully maintained, and their personal character, moral worth and religious hopes, so that unborn generations will arise and call them blessed.

www.ingramcontent.com/pod-product-compliance
Lightning Source LLC
Chambersburg PA
CBHW032137080426
42733CB00008B/1104